ESSENTIAL

Fast Pasta

p

Contents

Introduction

Pasta has existed in one form or another since the days of the Roman Empire. Yet Italy is not the only country to have a pasta-making tradition, countries as far afield as China, Mongolia, Greece, Spain, Israel and Russia share in the history of this culinary invention.

Nowadays pasta is a worldwide favourite and remains one of the most versatile ingredients in the kitchen. It can be combined with almost anything from meat to fish, vegetables to fruit and is especially delicious served with quick and simple herb sauces. No store cupboard should be without a supply of dried pasta, which combined with just a few ingredients can be turned into a mouth-watering and nutritious meal within minutes.

The variety of recipes in this book will appeal to all tastes, from the meat-lover to the vegetarian, yet all can be cooked quickly, fitting in with busy modern life-styles. Moreover, as the basic ingredient in every dish, pasta provides an excellent source of protein and carbohydrates, and it is easily incorporated into a low-fat diet.

 *Fast Pasta* shows how versatile pasta can be. The recipes range from traditional pasta dishes, such as Spaghetti alla Carbonara, to low-fat and vegetarian dishes, such as Pasta Provençal.

The variety of dishes include hearty main meals and also lighter recipes that make either an appetising side dish or a tasty lunch.

There is an enormous range of different types of pasta, many of which are available both dried and fresh. 200 different types of pasta are available in various shapes, sizes and colours. It is a good idea to have a supply of dried pasta, such as rigatoni, spaghetti or perhaps fusilli in your cupboard as these are quickly cooked. Alternatively you can buy fresh pasta from a delicatessens or supermarket.

Different pasta requires different cooking times and suit different types of sauce. It is generally considered best to use long ribbons, such as fettucine or tagliatelle with olive oil or a fresh tomato sauce, and bigger pasta, such as penne or fusilli, for meat sauce.

Perfect pasta relies on cooking time. Pasta should be cooked in lightly salted boiling water until it is tender yet firm to the bite. The Italians call this *al dente* (to the tooth). Dried unfilled pasta takes 8–12 minutes; fresh unfilled pasta takes 2–3 minutes; dried filled pasta takes 15–20 minutes; fresh filled pasta takes 8–10 minutes. To prevent sticking and to enhance flavour add a tablespoon of olive oil to the boiling water. Once the pasta is cooked, drain it in a colander and serve with sauce.

Goat's Cheese with Penne, Pear & Walnut Salad

Serves 4

INGREDIENTS

260 g/9 oz dried penne	2 ripe pears, cored and diced	1 small onion, sliced
5 tbsp olive oil	1 fresh basil sprig	1 large carrot, grated
1 head radicchio, torn into pieces	1 bunch of watercress, trimmed	250 g/9 oz goat's cheese, diced
1 Webbs lettuce, torn into pieces	2 tbsp lemon juice	salt and pepper
7 tbsp chopped walnuts	3 tbsp garlic vinegar	
	4 tomatoes, quartered	

1 Bring a large saucepan of lightly salted water to the boil. Add the penne and 1 tbsp of the olive oil and cook until tender, but still firm to the bite. Drain the pasta, refresh under cold running water, drain thoroughly again and set aside to cool.

2 Place the radicchio and Webbs lettuce in a large salad bowl and mix together well. Top with the pasta, walnuts, pears, basil and watercress.

3 Mix together the lemon juice, the remaining olive oil and the vinegar in a measuring jug (pitcher). Pour the mixture over the salad ingredients and toss to coat the salad leaves well.

4 Add the tomato quarters, onion slices, grated carrot and diced goat's cheese and toss together, using 2 forks, until well mixed. Leave the salad to chill in the refrigerator for about 1 hour before serving.

Patriotic Pasta

Serves 4

INGREDIENTS

460 g/1 lb/4 cups dried farfalle	460 g/1 lb cherry tomatoes	salt and pepper
4 tbsp olive oil	90 g/3 oz rocket (arugula)	Pecorino cheese, to garnish

1 Bring a large saucepan of lightly salted water to the boil. Add the farfalle and 1 tbsp of the olive oil and cook until tender, but still firm to the bite. Drain the farfalle thoroughly and return to the pan.

2 Cut the cherry tomatoes in half and trim the rocket (arugula).

3 Heat the remaining olive oil in a large saucepan. Add the tomatoes and cook for 1 minute. Add the farfalle and the rocket (arugula) and stir gently to mix. Heat through and season to taste with salt and black pepper.

4 Meanwhile, using a vegetable peeler, shave thin slices of Pecorino cheese.

5 Transfer the farfalle and vegetables to a warm serving dish. Garnish with the Pecorino cheese shavings and serve immediately.

COOK'S TIP

Pecorino cheese is a hard sheep's milk cheese which resembles Parmesan and is often used for grating over a variety of dishes. It has a sharp flavour and is only used in small quantities.

COOK'S TIP

Rocket (arugula) is a small plant with irregular-shaped leaves rather like those of turnip tops (greens). The flavour is distinctively peppery and slightly reminiscent of radish. It has always been popular in Italy, both in salads and for serving with pasta and has recently enjoyed a revival in Britain and the United States, where it has now become very fashionable.

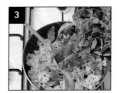

Pasta Niçoise Salad

Serves 4

INGREDIENTS

225 g/8 oz farfalle (bows)
175 g/6 oz French (green) beans, topped and tailed
350 g/12 oz fresh tuna steaks
115 g/4 oz baby plum tomatoes, halved
8 anchovy fillets, drained on absorbent kitchen paper

2 tbsp capers in brine, drained
25 g/1 oz pitted black olives in brine, drained
fresh basil leaves, to garnish
salt and pepper

DRESSING:
1 tbsp olive oil
1 garlic clove, crushed
1 tbsp lemon juice
½ tsp finely grated lemon rind
1 tbsp shredded fresh basil leaves

1 Cook the pasta in lightly salted boiling water according to the instructions on the packet until just cooked. Drain well, set aside and keep warm.

2 Bring a small saucepan of lightly salted water to the boil and cook the French (green) beans for 5–6 minutes until just tender. Drain well and toss into the pasta. Set aside and keep warm.

3 Preheat the grill (broiler) to medium. Rinse and pat the tuna steaks dry on absorbent kitchen paper. Season on both sides with black pepper. Place the tuna steaks on the grill (broiler) rack and cook for 4–5 minutes on each side until cooked through.

4 Drain the tuna on absorbent kitchen paper and flake into bite-sized pieces. Toss the tuna into the pasta along with the tomatoes, anchovies, capers and olives. Set aside and keep warm.

5 Meanwhile, prepare the dressing. Mix all the ingredients together and season with salt and pepper to taste. Pour the dressing over the pasta mixture and mix carefully. Transfer to a warmed serving bowl and serve sprinkled with fresh basil leaves.

Spaghetti alla Carbonara

Serves 4

INGREDIENTS

425 g/15 oz dried spaghetti
2 tbsp olive oil
1 large onion, thinly sliced
2 garlic cloves, chopped
175 g/6 oz rindless bacon, cut
   into thin strips

25 g/1 oz/2 tbsp butter
175 g/6 oz mushrooms, thinly
   sliced
300 ml/½ pint/1¼ cups double
   (heavy) cream
3 eggs, beaten

100 g /3½ oz/1 cup freshly
   grated Parmesan cheese,
   plus extra to serve
   (optional)
salt and pepper
fresh sage sprigs, to garnish

1 Warm a large serving dish or bowl. Bring a large pan of lightly salted water to the boil. Add the spaghetti and 1 tbsp of the oil and cook until tender, but still firm to the bite. Drain, return to the pan and keep warm.

2 Heat the remaining oil in a frying pan (skillet) over a medium heat. Add the onion and fry until it is transparent. Add the garlic and bacon and fry until the bacon is crisp. Transfer to the warm dish.

3 Melt the butter in the frying pan (skillet). Add the mushrooms and fry, stirring occasionally, for 3-4 minutes. Return the bacon mixture to the pan. Cover and keep warm.

4 Mix together the cream, eggs and cheese in a large bowl and then season to taste with salt and pepper.

5 Working very quickly, tip the spaghetti into the bacon and mushroom mixture and pour over the eggs. Toss the spaghetti quickly into the egg and cream mixture, using 2 forks. garnish and serve with extra grated Parmesan cheese, if using.

COOK'S TIP

The key to success with this recipe is not to overcook the egg. That is why it is important to keep all the ingredients hot enough just to cook the egg and to work rapidly to avoid scrambling it.

Smoked Ham Linguini

Serves 4

INGREDIENTS

450 g/1 lb dried linguini
450 g/1 lb broccoli florets
225g/8 oz Italian smoked ham

150 ml/¼ pint/⅝ cup Italian
Cheese Sauce (see Cook's
Tip, below right)

salt and pepper
Italian bread, to serve

1 Bring a large pan of lightly salted water to the boil. Add the linguini and broccoli florets and cook for 10 minutes, until the linguini is tender, but still firm to the bite.

2 Drain the linguini and broccoli thoroughly, set aside and keep warm.

3 Meanwhile, make the Italian Cheese Sauce (see Cook's Tip, right).

4 Using a sharp knife, cut the Italian smoked ham into thin strips. Toss the linguini, broccoli and ham into the Italian Cheese Sauce and gently warm through over a very low heat.

5 Transfer the pasta mixture to a warm serving dish. Sprinkle with black pepper and serve with Italian bread.

COOK'S TIP

There are many types of Italian bread which would be suitable to serve with this dish. Ciabatta is made with olive oil and is available plain and with different ingredients, such as olives or sun-dried tomatoes.

COOK'S TIP

For Italian Cheese Sauce, melt 2 tbsp butter in a pan. Stir in 25 g/1 oz/¼ cup plain (all purpose) flour and cook gently until the roux is crumbly in texture. Stir in 300 ml/½ pint/1¼ cups hot milk and cook for 15 minutes. Add a pinch of nutmeg, a pinch of dried thyme, 2 tbsp white wine vinegar. Season. Stir in 3 tbsp double (heavy) cream, 60 g/2 oz/½ cup grated Mozzarella, 60g/2 oz/ ⅔ cup grated Parmesan, 1 tsp English mustard and 2 tbsp soured cream.

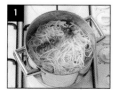

Chorizo & Wild Mushrooms with a Spicy Vermicelli

Serves 6

INGREDIENTS

680 g/1½ lb dried vermicelli
125 ml/4 fl oz/½ cup olive oil
2 garlic cloves
125 g/4½ oz chorizo, sliced

225 g/8 oz wild mushrooms
3 fresh red chillies, chopped
2 tbsp freshly grated
  Parmesan cheese

salt and pepper
10 anchovy fillets, to garnish

1 Bring a large pan of lightly salted water to the boil. Add the vermicelli and 1 tbsp of the oil and cook until just tender, but still firm to the bite. Drain, place on a warm serving plate and keep warm.

2 Meanwhile heat the remaining oil in a large frying pan (skillet). Add the garlic and fry for 1 minute. Add the chorizo and wild mushrooms and cook for 4 minutes, then add the chopped chillies and cook for 1 further minute.

3 Pour the chorizo and wild mushroom mixture over the vermicelli and season. Sprinkle over the freshly grated Parmesan cheese, garnish with a lattice of anchovy fillets and serve immediately.

VARIATION

Fresh sardines may be used instead of the anchovies. However, ensure that you gut and clean the sardines, removing the backbone, before using them.

COOK'S TIP

Always obtain wild mushrooms from a reliable source: never pick them yourself unless you are sure of their identity. Many varieties of mushrooms are now cultivated and most are indistinguishable from the wild varieties. Mixed colour oyster mushrooms are used here, but you could also use chanterelles. However, chanterelles shrink during cooking, so you may need more.

Pancetta & Pecorino Cakes on a Bed of Farfalle

Serves 4

INGREDIENTS

25 g/1 oz/2 tbsp butter, plus extra for greasing
100 g/3½ oz pancetta, rind removed
225 g/8 oz/2 cups self-raising (self-rising) flour

75 g/2 ¾ oz/⅞ cup grated pecorino cheese
150 ml/¼ pint/⅝ cup milk, plus extra for glazing
1 tbsp tomato ketchup
1 tsp Worcestershire sauce

400 g/14 oz/3½ cups dried farfalle
1 tbsp olive oil
salt and black pepper
3 tbsp Pesto (see page 74) or anchovy sauce (optional)
green salad, to serve

1 Grease a baking (cookie) sheet. Grill (broil) the pancetta until it is cooked, then allow it to cool and chop finely.

2 Sift the flour and a pinch of salt into a bowl. Rub in the butter with your fingertips, then add the pancetta and one-third of the grated cheese.

3 Mix together the milk, tomato ketchup and Worcestershire sauce and add to the dry ingredients, mixing to make a soft dough.

4 Roll out the dough on a lightly floured board to make a 18 cm/7 inch round. Brush with milk to glaze and cut into 8 wedges.

5 Arrange the dough wedges on the prepared baking (cookie) sheet and sprinkle over the remaining cheese. Bake in a preheated oven at 200°C/400°F/Gas 6 for 20 minutes.

6 Bring a pan of lightly salted water to the boil. Add the farfalle and the oil and cook until just tender, but still firm to the bite. Drain and transfer to a serving dish. Top with the pancetta and pecorino cakes. Serve with the sauce of your choice and a salad.

Orecchiette with Bacon & Tomatoes

Serves 4

INGREDIENTS

900 g/2 lb small, sweet
  tomatoes
6 slices rindless, smoked bacon
60 g/2 oz/4 tbsp butter
1 onion, chopped

1 garlic clove, crushed
4 fresh oregano sprigs,
  finely chopped
450 g/1 lb/4 cups dried
  orecchiette

1 tbsp olive oil
salt and pepper
freshly grated Pecorino
  cheese, to serve
fresh basil sprigs, to garnish

1 Blanch the tomatoes in boiling water. Drain, skin and seed the tomatoes, then roughly chop the flesh. Chop the bacon into small dices.

2 Melt the butter in a saucepan and fry the bacon until it is golden. Add the onion and garlic and fry for 5-7 minutes, until softened.

3 Add the tomatoes and oregano to the pan and season to taste. Lower the heat and simmer for 10-12 minutes.

4 Bring a pan of lightly salted water to the boil. Add the orecchiette and oil and cook for 12 minutes, until just tender, but still firm to the bite. Drain and transfer to a serving dish. Spoon over the bacon and tomato sauce and toss to coat. Garnish and serve.

VARIATION

You could also use 450 g/ 1 lb spicy Italian sausages. Squeeze the meat out of the skins and add to the pan in step 2 instead of the bacon.

COOK'S TIP

For an authentic Italian flavour use pancetta, rather than ordinary bacon. This kind of bacon is streaked with fat and adds rich undertones of flavour to many traditional dishes. It is available both smoked and unsmoked and can be bought in a single, large piece or cut into slices. You can buy it in some supermarkets and all Italian delicatessens.

Tagliarini with Gorgonzola

Serves 4

INGREDIENTS

25 g/1 oz/2 tbsp butter
225 g/8 oz Gorgonzola cheese,
    roughly crumbled
150 ml/¼ pint/⅝ cup double
    (heavy) cream

30 ml/2 tbsp dry white wine
1 tsp cornflour (cornstarch)
4 fresh sage sprigs, finely
    chopped
400 g/14 oz dried tagliarini

2 tbsp olive oil
salt and white pepper
fresh herb sprigs, to garnish

1 Melt the butter in a heavy-based saucepan. Stir in 175 g/6 oz of the Gorgonzola and melt, over a low heat, for 2 minutes.

2 Add the cream, wine and cornflour (cornstarch) and beat with a whisk until fully incorporated.

3 Stir in the sage and season to taste. Bring to the boil over a low heat, whisking constantly, until the sauce thickens. Remove from the heat and set aside.

4 Bring a large saucepan of lightly salted water to the boil. Add the tagliarini and 1 tbsp of the olive oil. Cook the pasta for 12–14 minutes or until just tender, drain thoroughly and toss in the remaining olive oil. Transfer the pasta to a serving dish and keep warm.

5 Reheat the sauce over a low heat, whisking constantly. Spoon the Gorgonzola sauce over the tagliarini, sprinkle over the remaining cheese, garnish and serve.

COOK'S TIP

Gorgonzola is one of the world's oldest veined cheeses and, arguably, its finest. When buying, always check that it is creamy yellow with delicate green veining. Avoid hard or discoloured cheese. It should have a rich, piquant aroma, not a bitter smell. If you find Gorgonzola too strong or rich, you could substitute Danish blue.

Pasta Omelette

Serves 2

INGREDIENTS

4 tbsp olive oil	1 tbsp chopped fresh flat leaf parsley	2 tbsp stuffed green olives, halved
1 small onion, chopped	pinch of chilli powder	salt and pepper
1 fennel bulb, thinly sliced	100 g/3¹/₂ oz cooked short pasta	fresh marjoram sprigs, to garnish
125 g/4¹/₂ oz potato, diced		
1 garlic clove, chopped		tomato salad, to serve
4 eggs		

1 Heat half the oil in a frying pan (skillet) and fry the onion, fennel and potato, stirring, for 8–10 minutes, until the potato is just tender.

2 Add the garlic and fry for 1 minute. Remove the pan from the heat and transfer the vegetables to a plate and set aside.

3 Beat the eggs until they are frothy. Stir in the parsley and season with salt, pepper and a pinch of chilli powder.

4 Heat 1 tbsp of the remaining oil in a clean frying pan (skillet). Add half of the egg mixture to the pan, then add the cooked vegetables, pasta and half of the olives. Pour in the remaining egg mixture and cook until the sides begin to set.

5 Lift up the edges of the omelette with a palette knife (spatula) to allow the uncooked egg to spread underneath. Cook until the underside is a light golden brown colour.

6 Slide the omelette out of the pan on to a plate. Wipe the pan with kitchen paper (kitchen towels) and heat the remaining oil. Invert the omelette into the pan and cook until the other side is golden brown.

7 Slide the omelette on to a warmed serving dish and garnish with the remaining olives and the fresh marjoram sprigs. Cut the omelette into wedges and serve with a tomato salad.

Spaghetti with Ricotta Cheese

Serves 4

INGREDIENTS

350 g/12 oz dried spaghetti
3 tbsp olive oil
40 g/¹⁄₂ oz/3 tbsp butter
2 tbsp chopped fresh flat leaf
   parsley
125 g/4¹⁄₂ oz/1 cup freshly
   ground almonds

125 g/4¹⁄₂ oz/¹⁄₂ cup ricotta
   cheese
pinch of grated nutmeg
pinch of ground cinnamon
150 ml/¹⁄₄ pint/⁵⁄₈ cup crème
   fraîche (unsweetened
   yogurt)

125 ml/4 fl oz hot chicken
   stock
1 tbsp pine nuts (kernels)
salt and pepper
fresh flat leaf parsley sprigs,
   to garnish

1 Bring a large pan of lightly salted water to the boil. Add the spaghetti and 1 tbsp of the oil and cook until tender, but still firm to the bite.

2 Drain the pasta, return to the pan and toss with the butter and chopped parsley. Set aside and keep warm.

3 To make the sauce, mix together the ground almonds, ricotta cheese, nutmeg, cinnamon and crème fraîche (unsweetened yogurt) over a low heat to form a thick paste. Stir in the remaining oil, then gradually stir in the hot chicken stock, until smooth. Season to taste.

4 Transfer the spaghetti to a warm serving dish, pour over the sauce and toss together well (see Cook's Tip, right). Sprinkle over the pine nuts (kernels), garnish with the flat leaf parsley sprigs and serve warm.

COOK'S TIP

Use two large forks to toss spaghetti or other long pasta, so that it is thoroughly coated with the sauce. Special spaghetti forks are available from some cookware departments and kitchen shops. Holding one fork in each hand, gently ease the prongs under the pasta on each side and lift them towards the centre. Continue until the pasta is completely coated.

Fettuccine with Anchovy & Spinach Sauce

Serves 4

INGREDIENTS

900 g/2 lb fresh, young
   spinach leaves
400 g/14 oz dried fettuccine

6 tbsp olive oil
3 tbsp pine nuts (kernels)
3 garlic cloves, crushed

8 canned anchovy fillets,
   drained and chopped
salt

1 Trim off any tough spinach stalks. Rinse the spinach leaves and place them in a large saucepan with only the water that is clinging to them after washing. Cover and cook over a high heat, shaking the pan occasionally, until the spinach has wilted, but retains its colour. Drain well, set aside and keep warm.

2 Bring a large saucepan of lightly salted water to the boil. Add the fettuccine and 1 tbsp of the oil and cook for 2–3 minutes until it is just tender, but still firm to the bite.

3 Heat 4 tbsp of the remaining oil in a saucepan. Add the pine nuts (kernels) and fry until golden. Remove from the pan and set aside.

4 Add the garlic to the pan and fry until golden. Add the anchovies and stir in the spinach. Cook, stirring, for 2-3 minutes, until heated through. Return the pine nuts (kernels) to the pan.

5 Drain the fettuccine, toss in the remaining olive oil and transfer to a warm serving dish. Spoon the anchovy and spinach sauce over the fettucine, toss lightly and serve immediately.

COOK'S TIP

If you are in a hurry, use frozen spinach. Thaw and drain it thoroughly, pressing out as much moisture as possible. Cut the leaves into strips and add to the dish with the anchovies in step 4.

Penne with Muscoli Fritti nell' Olio

Serves 4-6

INGREDIENTS

400/14 oz 3½ cups dried penne	1 tsp sea salt	TO GARNISH:
125 ml/4 fl oz/½ cup olive oil	90 g/3 oz/⅔ cup flour	1 lemon, thinly sliced
450 g/1 lb mussels, cooked and shelled	100 g/3½ oz sun-dried tomatoes, sliced	fresh basil leaves
	salt and pepper	

1 Bring a large pan of lightly salted water to the boil. Add the penne and 1 tbsp of the olive oil and cook until the pasta is just tender, but still firm to the bite.

2 Drain the pasta and place in a warm serving dish. Set aside and keep warm.

3 Sprinkle the mussels with the sea salt. Season the flour with salt and pepper, sprinkle into a bowl and toss the mussels in the flour until coated.

4 Heat the remaining oil in a frying pan (skillet) and fry the mussels until golden brown, stirring.

5 Toss the mussels with the penne and sprinkle with the sun-dried tomatoes. Garnish with lemon slices and basil leaves and serve.

VARIATION

You could substitute clams for the mussels. If using fresh clams, try smaller varieties, such as Venus.

COOK'S TIP

Sun-dried tomatoes have been used in Mediterranean countries for a long time, but have become popular elsewhere only quite recently. They are dried and then preserved in oil. They have a concentrated, almost roasted flavour and a dense texture. They should be drained and chopped or sliced before using.

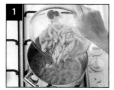

Creamed Strips of Sirloin with Rigatoni

Serves 4

INGREDIENTS

75 g/3 oz/6 tbsp butter
450 g/1 lb sirloin steak,
    trimmed and cut into thin
    strips
175 g/6 oz button
    mushrooms, sliced
1 tsp mustard

pinch of freshly grated root
    ginger
2 tbsp dry sherry
150 ml/¼ pint/⅝ cup double
    (heavy) cream
salt and pepper
4 slices hot toast, cut into
    triangles, to serve

PASTA:
450 g/1 lb dried rigatoni
2 tbsp olive oil
2 fresh basil sprigs
115 g/4 oz/8 tbsp butter

1 Melt the butter in a frying pan (skillet) and fry the steak over a low heat for 6 minutes. Transfer to an ovenproof dish and keep warm.

2 Add the mushrooms to the remaining juices in the frying pan (skillet) and cook for 2–3 minutes. Add the mustard, ginger, salt and pepper. Cook for 2 minutes, then add the sherry and cream. Cook for 3 minutes, then pour the cream sauce over the steak.

3 Bake the steak and cream mixture in a preheated oven at 90°C/ 375°F/Gas 5 for 10 minutes.

4 Bring a pan of lightly salted water to the boil. Add the rigatoni, olive oil and 1 basil sprig and boil for 10 minutes. Drain and transfer to a warm serving plate. Toss the pasta with the butter, garnish with the remaining basil sprig.

5 Serve the steak with the pasta and triangles of warm toast. Serve the rigatoni separately.

Egg Noodles with Beef

Serves 4

INGREDIENTS

285 g/10 oz egg noodles
3 tbsp walnut oil
2.5 cm/1 inch piece fresh root
ginger, cut into thin strips
5 spring onions (scallions),
finely shredded
2 garlic cloves, finely chopped

1 red (bell) pepper, cored,
seeded and thinly sliced
100 g/3½ oz button
mushrooms, thinly sliced
340 g/12 oz fillet steak, cut
into thin strips
1 tbsp cornflour (cornstarch)
5 tbsp dry sherry

3 tbsp soy sauce
1 tsp soft brown sugar
225 g/8 oz/1 cup beansprouts
1 tbsp sesame oil
salt and pepper
spring onion (scallion) strips,
to garnish

1 Bring a large saucepan of water to the boil. Add the noodles and cook according to the instructions on the packet. Drain and set aside.

2 Heat the walnut oil in a preheated wok. Add the ginger, spring onions (scallions) and garlic and stir-fry for 45 seconds. Add the (bell) pepper, mushrooms and steak and stir-fry for 4 minutes. Season to taste.

3 Mix together the cornflour (cornstarch), sherry and soy sauce in a small jug to form a paste, and pour into the wok. Sprinkle over the brown sugar and stir-fry all of the ingredients for 2 minutes.

4 Add the beansprouts, drained noodles and sesame oil to the wok, stir and toss together for 1 minute. Garnish with strips of spring onion (scallion) and serve.

COOK'S TIP

If you do not have a wok, you could prepare this dish in a frying pan (skillet). However, a wok is preferable, as the round base ensures an even distribution of heat and it is easier to keep stirring and tossing the contents when stir-frying.

Fettuccine with Fillet of Veal & Pink Grapefruit in a Rose Petal Butter Sauce

Serves 4

INGREDIENTS

450 g/1 lb dried fettuccine
7 tbsp olive oil
1 tsp chopped fresh oregano
1 tsp chopped fresh marjoram
170 g/6 oz/ ³/₄ cup butter
450 g/1 lb veal fillet, thinly
 sliced

150 ml/¹/₄ pint/⁵/₈ cup rose
 petal vinegar (see Cook's
 Tip, below)
150 ml/¹/₄ pint/⁵/₈ cup fish
 stock
50 ml/2 fl oz/ ¹/₄ cup grapefruit
 juice
50 ml/2 fl oz/¹/₄ cup double
 (heavy) cream

salt

TO GARNISH:
12 pink grapefruit segments
12 pink peppercorns
rose petals
fresh herb leaves

1 Cook the fettuccine with 1 tbsp of the oil in a pan of salted boiling water for 12 minutes. Drain and transfer to a warm serving dish, sprinkle over 2 tbsp of the olive oil, the oregano and marjoram.

2 Heat 50 g/2 oz/4 tbsp of the butter with the remaining oil in a frying pan (skillet) and cook the veal for 6 minutes. Spoon the veal on top of the pasta.

3 Add the vinegar and fish stock to the pan and boil vigorously until reduced by two thirds. Add the grapefruit juice and cream and simmer for 4 minutes. Dice the remaining butter and add to the pan, whisking until fully incorporated.

4 Pour the sauce around the veal, garnish and serve.

COOK'S TIP

To make rose petal vinegar, infuse the petals of 8 pesticide-free roses in 150 ml/¹/₄ pint/⁵/₈ cup white wine vinegar for 48 hours.

Stir-Fried Pork with Pasta & Vegetables

Serves 4

INGREDIENTS

3 tbsp sesame oil
350 g/12 oz pork fillet
   (tenderloin), cut into thin
   strips
450 g/1 lb dried taglioni
1 tbsp olive oil
8 shallots, sliced
2 garlic cloves, finely chopped

2.5 cm/1 inch piece fresh root
   ginger, grated
1 fresh green chilli, finely
   chopped
1 red (bell) pepper, cored,
   seeded and thinly sliced
1 green (bell) pepper, cored,
   seeded and thinly sliced

3 courgettes (zucchini), thinly
   sliced
2 tbsp ground almonds
1 tsp ground cinnamon
1 tbsp oyster sauce
60 g/2 oz creamed coconut
   (see Cook's Tip, below),
   grated
salt and pepper

1 Heat the sesame oil in a preheated wok. Season the pork and stir-fry for 5 minutes.

2 Bring a pan of salted water to the boil. Add the taglioni and olive oil and cook for 12 minutes. Set aside and keep warm.

3 Add the shallots, garlic, ginger and chilli to the wok and stir-fry for 2 minutes. Add the (bell) peppers and courgettes and stir-fry for 1 minute.

4 Add the ground almonds, cinnamon, oyster sauce and coconut cream to the wok and stir-fry for 1 minute.

5 Drain the taglioni and transfer to a serving dish. Top with the stir-fry and serve immediately.

COOK'S TIP

Creamed coconut is available from Chinese and Asian food stores and some large supermarkets. It is sold in compressed blocks and adds a concentrated coconut flavour to the dish.

Wholemeal (Whole Wheat) Spaghetti with Suprêmes of Chicken Nell Gwyn

Serves 4

INGREDIENTS

25 ml/1 fl oz/^{1}/8 cup rapeseed oil

3 tbsp olive oil

4 x 225 g/8 oz chicken suprêmes

150 ml/^{1}/4 pint/^{5}/8 cup orange brandy

15 g/^{1}/2 oz/2 tbsp plain (all purpose) flour

150 ml/^{1}/4 pint/^{5}/8 cup freshly squeezed orange juice

25 g/1 oz courgette (zucchini), cut into matchstick strips

25 g/1 oz red (bell) pepper, cut into matchstick strips

25 g/1 oz leek, finely shredded

400 g/14 oz dried wholemeal (whole wheat) spaghetti

3 large oranges, peeled and cut into segments

rind of 1 orange, cut into very fine strips

2 tbsp chopped fresh tarragon

150 ml/^{1}/4 pint/^{5}/8 cup fromage frais or ricotta cheese

salt and pepper

1 Heat the rapeseed oil and 1 tbsp of the olive oil in a frying pan (skillet). Add the chicken and cook quickly until golden brown. Add the orange brandy and cook for 3 minutes. Sprinkle over the flour and cook for 2 minutes.

2 Lower the heat and add the orange juice, courgette (zucchini), (bell) pepper and leek and season. Simmer for 5 minutes until the sauce has thickened.

3 Meanwhile, bring a pan of salted water to the boil. Add the spaghetti and 1 tbsp of the olive oil and cook for 10 minutes. Drain, transfer to a serving dish and drizzle over the remaining oil.

4 Add half the orange segments, half the orange rind, the tarragon and fromage frais or ricotta cheese to the sauce in the pan and cook for 3 minutes.

5 Place the chicken on top of the pasta, pour over a little sauce, garnish with orange segments and rind. Serve immediately.

Tagliatelle with Chicken Sauce

Serves 4

INGREDIENTS

250 g/9 oz fresh green
    tagliatelle
1 tbsp olive oil
fresh basil leaves, to garnish
salt

TOMATO SAUCE:
2 tbsp olive oil
1 small onion, chopped
1 garlic clove, chopped

400 g/14 oz can chopped
    tomatoes
2 tbsp chopped fresh parsley
1 tsp dried oregano
2 bay leaves
2 tbsp tomato purée (paste)
1 tsp sugar
salt and pepper

CHICKEN SAUCE:
60 g/2 oz/4 tbsp unsalted
    butter
400 g/14 oz boned chicken
    breasts, skinned and cut
    into thin strips
90 g/3 oz/ ³⁄₄ cup blanched
    almonds
300 ml/¹⁄₂ pint/1¹⁄₄ cups double
    (heavy) cream
salt and pepper

1 To make the tomato sauce, heat the oil and fry the onion until translucent. Add the garlic and fry for 1 minute. Stir in the tomatoes, herbs, tomato purée (paste), sugar and seasoning to taste. Bring to the boil and simmer for 15–20 minutes, until reduced by half. Remove from the heat and discard the bay leaves.

2 To make the chicken sauce, melt the butter in a frying pan (skillet) and stir-fry the chicken and almonds for 5–6 minutes, until the chicken is cooked.

3 Meanwhile, bring the cream to the boil over a low heat for about 10 minutes, until reduced by half. Pour the cream over the chicken and almonds,

stir and season to taste. Set aside and keep warm.

4 Bring a pan of salted water to the boil. Add the tagliatelle and olive oil and cook until tender. Drain and transfer to a warm serving dish. Spoon over the tomato sauce and arrange the chicken sauce on top. Garnish with the basil leaves and serve.

Cannelloni Filetti di Sogliola

Serves 6

INGREDIENTS

12 small fillets of sole
(about 115 g/4 oz each)
150 ml/¼ pint/⅝ cup red wine
90 g/3 oz/6 tbsp butter
115 g/4 oz/3⅞ cups sliced
button mushrooms
4 shallots, finely chopped

115 g/4 oz tomatoes, chopped
2 tbsp tomato purée (paste)
60 g/2 oz/½ cup plain (all
purpose) flour, sifted
150 ml/¼ pint/⅝ cup of
warm milk
2 tbsp double (heavy) cream

6 dried cannelloni tubes
175 g/6 oz cooked, peeled
prawns (shrimp), preferably
freshwater
salt and pepper
1 fresh dill sprig, to garnish

---

1 Brush the fillets with a little wine. Season and roll up, skin side inwards. Secure with a skewer or cocktail stick (toothpick).

2 Arrange the fish rolls in a single layer in a large frying pan (skillet), add the remaining red wine and poach for 4 minutes. Remove from the pan and reserve the cooking liquid.

3 Melt the butter in another pan. Fry the mushrooms and shallots for 2 minutes, then add the tomatoes and tomato purée (paste). Season the flour and stir it into the pan. Stir in the reserved cooking liquid and half the milk. Cook over a low heat, stirring, for 4 minutes. Remove from the heat and stir in the cream.

4 Bring a pan of salted water to the boil. Add the cannelloni and cook for 8 minutes, until tender but still firm to the bite. Drain and set aside to cool.

5 Remove the skewers or cocktail sticks from the fish rolls. Put 2 sole fillets into each cannelloni tube with 3–4 prawns (shrimp) and a little red wine sauce. Arrange the cannelloni in an ovenproof dish, pour over the sauce and bake in a preheated oven at 200°C/ 400°F/ Gas 6 for 20 minutes.

6 Serve the cannelloni with the red wine sauce, garnished with a sprig of dill.

Red Mullet Fillets with Orecchiette, Amaretto & Orange Sauce

Serves 4

INGREDIENTS
---

90 g/3 oz/3 ¾ cup plain
   (all purpose) flour
8 red mullet fillets
25 g/1 oz/2 tbsp butter
150 ml/¼ pint/⅝ cup fish
   stock
1 tbsp crushed almonds
1 tsp pink peppercorns

1 orange, peeled and cut
   into segments
1 tbsp orange liqueur
grated rind of 1 orange
450 g/1 lb dried orecchiette
1 tbsp olive oil
150 ml/¼ pint/⅝ cup double
   (heavy) cream

4 tbsp amaretto
salt and pepper

TO GARNISH:
2 tbsp snipped fresh chives
1 tbsp toasted almonds

---

1 Season the flour and sprinkle into a shallow bowl. Press the fish fillets into the flour to coat. Melt the butter in a frying pan (skillet) and fry the fish over a low heat for 3 minutes, until browned.

2 Add the fish stock to the pan and cook for 4 minutes. Carefully remove the fish, cover with foil and keep warm.

3 Add the almonds, pink peppercorns, half the orange, the orange liqueur and orange rind to the pan. Simmer until the liquid has reduced by half.

4 Meanwhile, bring a large saucepan of lightly salted water to the boil. Add the orecchiette and olive oil and cook for 15 minutes, until tender but still firm to the bite.

5 Season the sauce and stir in the cream and amaretto. Cook for 2 minutes. Coat the fish with the sauce in the pan.

6 Drain the pasta and transfer to a serving dish. Top with the fish fillets and their sauce. Garnish with the remaining orange segments, the chives and toasted almonds. Serve.

Spaghetti al Tonno

Serves 4

INGREDIENTS

200 g/7 oz can tuna, drained
60 g/2 oz can anchovies,
    drained
250 ml/9 fl oz/1⅛ cups
    olive oil

60 g/2 oz/1 cup roughly
    chopped flat leaf parsley,
    plus extra to garnish
150 ml/¼ pint/⅝ cup crème
    fraîche

450 g/1 lb dried spaghetti
25 g/1 oz/2 tbsp butter
salt and pepper
black olives, to garnish
crusty bread, to serve

1 Remove any bones
from the tuna. Put the
tuna into a food processor
or blender, together with
the anchovies, 225 ml/
8 fl oz/1 cup of the olive oil
and the flat leaf parsley.
Process until smooth.

2 Spoon the crème
fraîche into the food
processor or blender and
process again for a few
seconds to blend thoroughly.
Season to taste.

3 Bring a large pan of
lightly salted water to
the boil. Add the spaghetti

and the remaining olive oil
and cook until tender, but
still firm to the bite.

4 Drain the spaghetti,
return to the pan and
place over a medium heat.
Add the butter and toss
well to coat. Spoon in the
sauce and toss into
the spaghetti, using 2 forks.

5 Remove the pan from
the heat and divide the
spaghetti between 4 warm
individual serving plates.
Garnish with olives and
parsley and serve with
warm, crusty bread.

VARIATION

*If liked, you could add
1–2 garlic cloves to the
sauce, substitute 25 g/
1 oz/½ cup chopped fresh
basil for half the parsley and
garnish with capers instead
of black olives.*

Spaghetti with Seafood Sauce

Serves 4

INGREDIENTS

225 g/8 oz dried spaghetti,
broken into 15 cm/6 inch
lengths
2 tbsp olive oil
300 ml/^{1}/$_2$ pint/1^1/$_4$ cups
chicken stock
1 tsp lemon juice
1 small cauliflower, cut into
florets (flowerets)
2 carrots, thinly sliced

115 g/4 oz mangetouts (snow
peas)
60 g/2 oz/4 tbsp butter
1 onion, sliced
225 g/8 oz courgettes
(zucchini), sliced
1 garlic clove, chopped
350 g/12 oz frozen, cooked,
peeled prawns (shrimp),
defrosted

2 tbsp chopped fresh parsley
25 g/1 oz/^{1}/$_3$ cup freshly grated
Parmesan cheese
^{1}/$_2$ tsp paprika
salt and pepper
4 unpeeled, cooked prawns
(shrimp), to garnish

1 Bring a pan of lightly salted water to the boil. Add the spaghetti and 1 tbsp of the olive oil and cook until tender, but still firm to the bite. Drain, toss with the remaining olive oil, cover and keep warm.

2 Bring the chicken stock and lemon juice to the boil. Add the cauliflower and carrots and cook for 3–4 minutes.

Remove from the pan and set aside. Cook the mangetouts (snow peas) for 1–2 minutes then set aside with the other vegetables.

3 Melt half the butter in a frying pan (skillet) and fry the onion and courgettes (zucchini) for 3 minutes. Add the garlic and prawns (shrimp) and cook for a further 2–3 minutes. Stir in the

reserved vegetables and heat through. Season to taste and stir in the remaining butter.

4 Transfer the spaghetti to a warm serving dish. Mix in the sauce and the chopped parsley until coated. Sprinkle over the Parmesan cheese and paprika, garnish with the unpeeled prawns (shrimp) and serve immediately.

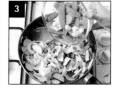

Pasta Shells with Mussels

Serves 4-6

INGREDIENTS

1.25 kg/2 ¾ lb mussels
225 ml/8 fl oz/1 cup dry white wine
2 large onions, chopped
115 g/4 oz/½ cup unsalted butter

6 large garlic cloves, finely chopped
5 tbsp chopped fresh parsley
300 ml/½ pint/1¼ cups double (heavy) cream
400 g/14 oz dried pasta shells

1 tbsp olive oil
salt and pepper
crusty bread, to serve

1 Scrub and debeard the mussels under cold running water. Discard any that do not close immediately when tapped. Put the mussels in a pan with the wine and half of the onions. Cover and cook over a medium heat, shaking the pan frequently, until the shells open.

2 Remove from the heat. Drain the mussels and reserve the cooking liquid. Discard any mussels that have not opened. Strain the cooking liquid and reserve.

3 Fry the remaining onion in the butter for 2–3 minutes. Stir in the garlic and cook for 1 minute. Gradually stir in the reserved cooking liquid, parsley and cream. Season and leave to simmer.

4 Cook the pasta with the oil in a pan of salted water until just tender, but still firm to the bite. Drain, return to the pan, cover and keep warm.

5 Reserve a few mussels for the garnish and remove the remainder from their shells. Stir the shelled mussels into the cream sauce and warm briefly. Transfer the pasta to a serving dish. Pour over the sauce and toss well to coat. Garnish with the reserved mussels and serve with warm, crusty bread.

COOK'S TIP

Pasta shells are ideal because the sauce collects in the cavities and impregnates the pasta with flavour.

Vermicelli with Clams

Serves 4

INGREDIENTS

400 g/14 oz dried vermicelli,
   spaghetti or other long
   pasta
2 tbsp olive oil
25 g/1 oz/2 tbsp butter
2 onions, chopped
2 garlic cloves, chopped

2 x 200 g/7 oz jars clams in
   brine
125 ml/4 fl oz/¹/₂ cup white
   wine
4 tbsp chopped fresh parsley
¹/₂ tsp dried oregano
pinch of freshly grated nutmeg

salt and pepper

TO GARNISH:
fresh basil sprigs

1 Bring a large pan of lightly salted water to the boil. Add the pasta and half the olive oil and cook until tender, but still firm to the bite. Drain, return to the pan and add the butter. Cover the pan, shake well and keep warm.

2 Heat the remaining oil in a saucepan over a medium heat. Add the onions and fry until they are translucent. Stir in the garlic and cook for 1 minute.

3 Strain the liquid from 1 jar of clams and add the liquid to the pan, together with the wine. Stir, bring to simmering point and simmer for 3 minutes. Drain the second jar of clams and discard the liquid.

4 Add the clams, parsley and oregano to the saucepan and season with pepper and nutmeg. Lower the heat and cook until the sauce is completely heated through.

5 Transfer the pasta to a serving dish and pour over the sauce. Garnish with the basil and serve.

COOK'S TIP

There are many different types of clams found along almost every coast in the world. Those traditionally used in this dish are the tiny ones – only 2.5–5 cm/ 1–2 inches across – known in Italy as vongole.

Spaghetti with Smoked Salmon

Serves 4

INGREDIENTS

450 g/1 lb dried buckwheat
  spaghetti
2 tbsp olive oil
90 g/3 oz/$^1/_2$ cup crumbled
  feta cheese
salt

fresh coriander (cilantro) or
  parsley leaves, to garnish

SAUCE:
300 ml/$^1/_2$ pint/1$^1/_4$ cups double
  (heavy) cream
150 ml/$^1/_4$ pint/$^5/_8$ cup whisky or
  brandy

125 g/4$^1/_2$ oz smoked salmon
pinch of cayenne pepper
black pepper
2 tbsp chopped fresh coriander
  (cilantro) or parsley

1 Bring a large pan of lightly salted water to the boil. Add the spaghetti and 1 tbsp of the olive oil and cook until tender, but still firm to the bite. Drain and return to the pan with the remaining olive oil. Cover, set aside and keep warm.

2 Pour the cream into a small saucepan and bring to simmering point, but do not let it boil. Pour the whisky or brandy into another small saucepan and bring to simmering point, but do not allow it to boil. Remove both pans from the heat and mix together the cream and whisky or brandy.

3 Cut the smoked salmon into thin strips and add to the cream mixture. Season with cayenne and black pepper. Just before serving, stir in the fresh coriander (cilantro) or parsley.

4 Transfer the spaghetti to a warm serving dish, pour over the sauce and toss thoroughly with 2 large forks. Scatter over the crumbled feta cheese, garnish with the coriander (cilantro) or parsley leaves and serve immediately.

COOK'S TIP

Serve this rich and luxurious dish with a green salad tossed in a lemony dressing.

Fettuccine all'Alfredo

Serves 4

INGREDIENTS

25 g/1 oz/2 tbsp butter
200 ml/7 fl oz/⁷⁄₈ cup double
   (heavy) cream
460 g/1 lb fresh fettuccine

1 tbsp olive oil
90 g/3 oz/1 cup freshly grated
   Parmesan cheese, plus
   extra to serve

pinch of freshly grated
   nutmeg
salt and pepper
fresh parsley sprigs, to garnish

1 Put the butter and 150 ml/¼ pint/⁵⁄₈ cup of the cream in a large saucepan and bring the mixture to the boil over a medium heat. Reduce the heat and then simmer gently for about 1½ minutes, or until slightly thickened.

2 Meanwhile, bring a large pan of lightly salted water to the boil. Add the fettuccine and olive oil and cook for 2–3 minutes, until tender but still firm to the bite. Drain the fettuccine, then pour over the cream sauce.

3 Using 2 forks, toss the fettuccine in the sauce over a low heat until thoroughly coated.

4 Add the remaining cream, the Parmesan cheese and nutmeg to the fettuccine mixture and season to taste. Toss thoroughly to coat while gently heating through.

5 Transfer the fettucine mixture to a warm serving plate and garnish with the fresh parsley sprigs. Serve immediately, handing extra grated Parmesan cheese separately.

VARIATION

This classic Roman dish is often served with the addition of strips of ham and fresh peas. Add 225 g/ 8 oz/2 cups shelled cooked peas and 175 g/6 oz ham strips with the Parmesan cheese in step 4.

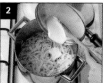

Creamy Pasta & Broccoli

Serves 4

INGREDIENTS

60 g/2 oz/4 tbsp butter
1 large onion, finely chopped
450 g/1 lb dried ribbon pasta
460 g/1 lb broccoli, broken
　into florets (flowerets)

150 ml/¹/₄ pint/⁵/₈ cup boiling
　vegetable stock
1 tbsp plain (all purpose) flour
150 ml/¹/₄ pint/⁵/₈ cup single
　(light) cream

60 g/2 oz/¹/₂ cup grated
　mozzarella cheese
freshly grated nutmeg
salt and white pepper
fresh apple slices, to garnish

1 Melt half of the butter in a large saucepan over a medium heat. Add the onion and fry for 4 minutes.

2 Add the pasta and broccoli to the pan and cook, stirring constantly, for 2 minutes. Add the vegetable stock, bring back to the boil and simmer for a further 12 minutes. Season well with salt and white pepper.

3 Meanwhile, melt the remaining butter in a saucepan over a medium heat. Stir in the flour and cook for 2 minutes. Gradually stir in the cream and bring to simmering point, but do not boil. Add the grated cheese and season with salt and a little freshly grated nutmeg.

4 Drain the pasta and broccoli mixture and pour over the cheese sauce. Cook, stirring occasionally, for about 2 minutes. Transfer the pasta and broccoli mixture to a warm, large, deep serving dish and serve garnished with slices of fresh apple.

VARIATION

This dish would also be delicious and look just as colourful made with Cape broccoli, which is actually a purple variety of cauliflower and not broccoli at all.

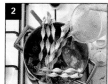

Green Tagliatelle with Garlic

Serves 4

INGREDIENTS

2 tbsp walnut oil
1 bunch spring onions
    (scallions), sliced
2 garlic cloves, thinly sliced
250 g/8 oz/3¼ cups sliced
    mushrooms
450 g/1 lb fresh green and
    white tagliatelle

1 tbsp olive oil
225 g/8 oz frozen spinach,
    thawed and drained
115 g/4 oz/½ cup full-fat soft
    cheese with garlic and
    herbs
4 tbsp single (light) cream

60 g/2 oz/½ cup chopped,
    unsalted pistachio nuts
2 tbsp shredded fresh basil
salt and pepper
fresh basil sprigs, to garnish
Italian bread, to serve

1 Heat the walnut oil in a large frying pan (skillet). Add the spring onions (scallions) and garlic and fry for 1 minute, until just softened.

2 Add the mushrooms to the pan, stir well, cover and cook over a low heat for about 5 minutes, until softened.

3 Meanwhile, bring a large saucepan of lightly salted water to the boil. Add the tagliatelle and olive oil and cook for 3–5 minutes, until tender but still firm to the bite. Drain and return to the saucepan.

4 Add the spinach to the frying pan (skillet) and heat through for 1–2 minutes. Add the cheese to the pan and allow to melt slightly. Stir in the cream and continue to cook, without allowing the mixture to come to the boil, until warmed through.

5 Pour the sauce over the tagliatelle, season with salt and black pepper to taste and mix well. Heat through gently, stirring constantly, for 2–3 minutes.

6 Transfer the pasta to a serving dish and sprinkle with the pistachio nuts and shredded basil. Garnish with the basil sprigs and serve with the Italian bread of your choice.

Spaghetti Olio e Aglio

Serves 4

INGREDIENTS

125 ml/4 fl oz/¹⁄₂ cup olive oil
3 garlic cloves, crushed
460 g/1 lb fresh spaghetti

3 tbsp roughly chopped fresh
  parsley

salt and pepper

1 Reserve 1 tbsp of the olive oil and heat the remainder in a medium saucepan. Add the garlic and a pinch of salt and cook over a low heat, stirring constantly, until golden brown, then remove the pan from the heat. Do not allow the garlic to burn as it will taint its flavour. (If it does burn, you will have to start all over again!)

2 Meanwhile, bring a large saucepan of lightly salted water to the boil. Add the spaghetti and remaining olive oil and cook for 2–3 minutes, until tender, but still firm to the bite. Drain the spaghetti thoroughly and return to the pan.

3 Add the oil and garlic mixture to the spaghetti and toss to coat thoroughly. Season with pepper, add the chopped fresh parsley and toss to coat again.

4 Transfer the spaghetti to a warm serving dish and serve immediately.

COOK'S TIP

It is worth buying the best-quality olive oil for dishes such as this one which makes a feature of its flavour. Extra virgin oil is produced from the first pressing and has the lowest acidity. It is more expensive than other types of olive oil, but has the finest flavour. Virgin olive oil is slightly more acid, but is also well flavoured. Oil simply labelled pure has usually been heat-treated and refined by mechanical means and, consequently, lacks character and flavour.

Mediterranean Spaghetti

Serves 4

INGREDIENTS

2 tbsp olive oil
1 large, red onion, chopped
2 garlic cloves, crushed
1 tbsp lemon juice
4 baby aubergines (eggplants), quartered

600 ml/1 pint/2½ cups passata (sieved tomatoes)
2 tsp caster (superfine) sugar
2 tbsp tomato purée (paste)
400 g/14 oz can artichoke hearts, drained and halved

115 g/4 oz/1 cup stoned (pitted) black olives
350 g/12 oz dried spaghetti
25 g/1 oz/2 tbsp butter
salt and pepper
fresh basil sprigs, to garnish
olive bread, to serve

1 Heat 1 tbsp of the olive oil in a large frying pan (skillet). Add the onion, garlic, lemon juice and aubergines (eggplants) and cook over a low heat for 4–5 minutes, until the onion and aubergines (eggplants) are lightly golden brown.

2 Pour in the passata (sieved tomatoes), season to taste with salt and black pepper and stir in the caster (superfine) sugar and tomato purée (paste). Bring to the boil, then simmer, stirring occasionally, for 20 minutes.

3 Gently stir in the artichoke hearts and black olives and cook for 5 minutes.

4 Meanwhile, bring a large saucepan of lightly salted water to the boil. Add the spaghetti and the remaining oil and cook for 7–8 minutes, until tender but still firm to the bite.

5 Drain the spaghetti thoroughly and toss with the butter. Transfer the spaghetti to a large serving dish.

6 Pour the vegetable sauce over the spaghetti, garnish with the sprigs of fresh basil and serve immediately with olive bread.

Creamed Spaghetti & Mushrooms

Serves 4

INGREDIENTS

60 g/2 oz/4 tbsp butter
2 tbsp olive oil
6 shallots, sliced
450 g/1 lb/6 cups sliced
   button mushrooms
1 tsp plain (all purpose) flour

150 ml/¼ pint/⅝ cup double
   (heavy) cream
2 tbsp port
115 g/4 oz sun-dried
   tomatoes, chopped
freshly grated nutmeg

450g /1 lb dried spaghetti
1 tbsp freshly chopped parsley
salt and pepper
6 triangles of fried white
   bread, to serve

1 Heat the butter and
1 tbsp of the oil in a
large pan. Add the shallots
and cook over a medium
heat for 3 minutes. Add the
mushrooms and cook over
a low heat for 2 minutes.
Season with salt and black
pepper, sprinkle over the
flour and cook, stirring
constantly, for 1 minute.

2 Gradually stir in the
cream and port, add
the sun-dried tomatoes and
a pinch of grated nutmeg
and cook over a low heat
for 8 minutes.

3 Bring a large saucepan
of lightly salted
water to the boil. Add the
spaghetti and remaining
olive oil and cook for
12–14 minutes, until tender
but still firm to the bite.

4 Drain the spaghetti and
return to the pan. Pour
over the mushroom sauce
and cook for 3 minutes.
Transfer the spaghetti and
mushroom sauce to a large
serving plate and sprinkle
over the chopped parsley.
Serve with crispy triangles
of fried bread.

VARIATION

*Non-vegetarians could add
115 g/4 oz Parma ham
(prosciutto), cut into thin
strips and heated gently in
25 g/1 oz/2 tbsp butter, to
the pasta along with the
mushroom sauce.*

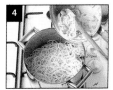

Spicy Tomato Tagliatelle

Serves 4

INGREDIENTS

50 g/1 ³/₄ oz/3 tbsp butter
1 onion, finely chopped
1 garlic clove, crushed
2 small red chillies, deseeded
  and diced

450 g/1 lb fresh tomatoes,
  skinned, deseeded and diced
200 ml/7 fl oz/³/₄ cup vegetable
  stock
2 tbsp tomato purée

1 tsp sugar
salt and pepper
675 g/1¹/₂ lb fresh green and
  white tagliatelle, or 350 g/
  12 oz dried

1 Melt the butter in a large saucepan. Add the onion and garlic and cook for 3–4 minutes or until softened.

2 Add the chillies to the pan and continue cooking for about 2 minutes.

3 Add the tomatoes and stock, reduce the heat and leave to simmer for 10 minutes, stirring.

4 Pour the sauce into a food processor and blend for 1 minute until smooth. Alternatively, push the sauce through a sieve.

5 Return the sauce to the pan and add the tomato purée, sugar, and salt and pepper to taste. Gently reheat over a low heat, until piping hot.

6 Cook the tagliatelle in a pan of boiling water according to the instructions on the packet or until it is cooked, but still has 'bite'. Drain the tagliatelle, transfer to serving plates and serve with the tomato sauce.

VARIATION

Try topping your pasta dish with 50 g/1¹/₄ oz pancetta or unsmoked bacon, diced and dry-fried for 5 minutes until crispy.

Basil & Tomato Pasta

Serves 4

INGREDIENTS

1 tbsp olive oil	450 g/1 lb tomatoes, halved	salt and pepper
2 sprigs rosemary	1 tbsp sun-dried tomato paste	675 g/1½ lb fresh farfalle or
2 cloves garlic, unpeeled	12 fresh basil leaves, plus	350 g/12 oz dried farfalle
	extra to garnish	

1 Place the oil, rosemary, garlic and tomatoes, skin side up, in a shallow roasting tin (pan).

2 Drizzle with a little oil and cook under a preheated grill (broiler) for 20 minutes or until the tomato skins are slightly charred.

3 Peel the skin from the tomatoes. Roughly chop the tomato flesh and place in a pan.

4 Squeeze the pulp from the garlic cloves and mix with the tomato flesh and sun-dried tomato paste.

5 Roughly tear the fresh basil leaves into smaller pieces and then stir them into the sauce. Season with a little salt and pepper to taste.

6 Cook the farfalle in a saucepan of boiling water according to the instructions on the packet or until it is cooked through, but still has 'bite'. Drain.

7 Gently heat the tomato and basil sauce.

8 Transfer the farfalle to serving plates and serve with the basil and tomato sauce.

COOK'S TIP

This sauce tastes just as good when served cold in a pasta salad.

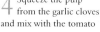

Basil & Pine Nut Pesto

Serves 4

INGREDIENTS

about 40 fresh basil leaves,
washed and dried
3 garlic cloves, crushed
25 g/1 oz pine nuts

50 g/1 ³/₄ oz Parmesan cheese,
finely grated
2–3 tbsp extra virgin olive oil
salt and pepper

675 g/1¹/₂ lb fresh pasta or
350 g/12 oz dried pasta

1 Rinse the basil leaves and pat them dry with paper towels.

2 Put the basil leaves, garlic, pine nuts and grated Parmesan into a food processor and blend for about 30 seconds or until smooth. Alternatively, pound the ingredients by hand, using a mortar and pestle.

3 If you are using a food processor, keep the motor running and slowly add the olive oil. Alternatively, add the oil drop by drop while stirring briskly. Season with salt and pepper.

4 Meanwhile, cook the pasta in a saucepan of boiling water according to the instructions on the packet or until it is cooked through, but still has 'bite'. Drain.

5 Transfer the pasta to a serving plate and serve with the pesto. Toss to mix well and serve hot.

COOK'S TIP

You can store pesto in the refrigerator for about 4 weeks. Cover the surface of the pesto with olive oil before sealing the container or bottle, to prevent the basil from oxidising and turning black.

VARIATION

Try making a walnut version of this pesto. Substitute 25 g/1 oz walnuts for the pine nuts and add 1 tablespoon walnut oil in step 2.

Pasta Provençale

Serves 4

INGREDIENTS

225 g/8 oz penne (quills)
1 tbsp olive oil
25 g/1 oz pitted black olives, drained and chopped
25 g/1 oz dry-pack sun-dried tomatoes, soaked, drained and chopped
400 g/14 oz can artichoke hearts, drained and halved

115 g/4 oz baby courgettes (zucchini), trimmed and sliced
115 g/4 oz baby plum tomatoes, halved
100 g/3½ oz assorted baby salad leaves
salt and pepper
shredded basil leaves, to garnish

DRESSING:
4 tbsp passata (sieved tomatoes)
2 tbsp low-fat natural fromage frais (unsweetened yogurt)
1 tbsp unsweetened orange juice
1 small bunch fresh basil, shredded

1 Cook the penne (quills) according to the instructions on the packet. Do not overcook the pasta – it should still have 'bite'. Drain well and return to the pan. Stir in the olive oil, salt and pepper, olives and sun-dried tomatoes. Leave to cool.

2 Gently mix the artichokes, courgettes (zucchini) and plum tomatoes into the cooked pasta. Arrange the salad leaves in a serving bowl.

3 To make the dressing, mix all the ingredients together and toss into the vegetables and pasta.

4 Spoon the mixture on top of the salad leaves and garnish with shredded basil leaves.

VARIATION

For a non-vegetarian version, stir 225 g/8 oz canned tuna in brine, drained and flaked, into the pasta together with the vegetables. Other pasta shapes can be included – look out for farfalle (bows) and rotelle (spoked wheels).

Vegetable Spaghetti with Lemon Dressing

Serves 4

INGREDIENTS

225 g/8 oz celeriac
2 medium carrots
2 medium leeks
1 small red (bell) pepper
1 small yellow (bell) pepper
2 garlic cloves
1 tsp celery seeds

1 tbsp lemon juice
300 g/10½ oz spaghetti
celery leaves, chopped, to
  garnish

LEMON DRESSING:
1 tsp finely grated lemon rind

1 tbsp lemon juice
4 tbsp low-fat natural
  fromage frais
  (unsweetened yogurt)
salt and pepper
2 tbsp snipped fresh chives

1 Peel the celeriac and carrots, cut into thin matchsticks and place in a bowl. Slice the leeks, rinse to flush out any trapped dirt, then shred finely. Halve, deseed and slice the (bell) peppers. Peel and thinly slice the garlic. Add these vegetables to the celeriac and the carrots.

2 Toss the vegetables with the celery seeds and lemon juice.

3 Bring a large pan of water to the boil and cook the spaghetti according to the instructions on the packet. Drain well and keep warm.

4 Bring another large saucepan of water to the boil, put the vegetables in a steamer or sieve (strainer) and place over the boiling water. Cover and steam for 6–7 minutes or until just tender.

5 When the spaghetti and vegetables are cooked, mix the ingredients for the lemon dressing together.

6 Transfer the spaghetti and vegetables to a warm serving bowl and mix with the dressing. Garnish with chopped celery leaves and serve.

This is a Parragon Book
First published in 2000

Parragon
Queen Street House
4 Queen Street
Bath BA1 1HE, UK

ISBN: 0-75253-618-4

Printed in China

Note

Cup measurements in this book are for American cups. Tablespoons are assumed to be
15 ml. Unless otherwise stated, milk is assumed to be full fat, eggs are medium and
pepper is freshly ground black pepper.